Getting Over a Breakup

How to Heal a Broken Heart (An Eight Step Guide)

by Anne Willoughby

Table of Contents

Introduction 1

Step 1: How to Understand the Suffering 7

Step 2: How to Break Away, and Why You Must 11

Step 3: How to Let Yourself Feel 15

Step 4: How to Stop Blaming Yourself 19

Step 5: How to Let Out Aggression, then Calm Down 23

Step 6: How to Fill the Void 29

Step 7: How to Address Your Flaws 33

Step 8: How to Get Your Social Life Back on Track 37

Conclusion 41

Introduction

Well, the worst that you feared has finally come to pass — you've been through a breakup and are now trying to find ways to heal your broken heart.

Let's start with a few things: first, the thing that you feared the most has come and gone, and you're still here. Take this as the first sign towards resilience and self-revival. You've been through it, and while it may have hurt you, *you're still here*.

Second, you're not alone. Thousands (*thousands!*) of others, if not more, are going through it alongside you **right now** — the same pain, angst, fears and worries. This revelation isn't to showcase some pessimistic downside to modern dating, but rather to address the pity party that most of us go through in times like these.

Third, the very fact that you're reading this means that you're trying to find ways to cope with and manage your feelings. That's an *excellent* sign in and of itself. The fact that you're reading a guide on "How to Heal" also means that somewhere inside, even if you haven't accepted it yourself, you want to move on from the relationship instead of clinging to history.

But, the problem is that everything you've read so far about getting over a breakup seems to give snippets of incomplete advice without context. And these so-called experts often contradict each other. Stay busy, don't stay busy. Talk to your ex, don't talk to your ex. Seek closure, stay far away. All of them are confusing and generic, and frankly, very few of them are genuinely helpful. And *that* is why I've written this book.

So, are you ready to get through healing your heart like a *boss*? Are you ready to come out on the other side *stronger than ever before*? Let's begin!

© Copyright 2014 by LCPublifish LLC - All rights reserved.

This document is geared towards providing reliable information in regards to the topic and issue covered. The publication is sold with the idea that the publisher is not required to render accounting, officially permitted, or otherwise, qualified services. If advice is necessary, legal or professional, a practiced individual in the profession should be ordered.

- From a Declaration of Principles which was accepted and approved equally by a Committee of the American Bar Association and a Committee of Publishers and Associations.

In no way is it legal to reproduce, duplicate, or transmit any part of this document in either electronic means or in printed format. Recording of this publication is strictly prohibited and any storage of this document is not allowed unless with written permission from the publisher. All rights reserved.

The information provided herein is stated to be truthful and consistent, in that any liability, in terms of inattention or otherwise, by any usage or abuse of any policies, processes, or directions contained within is solely and completely the responsibility of the recipient reader. Under no circumstances will any legal responsibility or blame be held against the publisher for any reparation, damages, or monetary loss due to the information herein, either directly or indirectly.

Respective authors own all copyrights not held by the publisher.

The information herein is offered for informational purposes solely, and is universal as so. The presentation of the information is without contract or any type of guarantee assurance.

The trademarks that are used are without any consent, and the publication of the trademark is without permission or backing by the trademark owner. All trademarks and brands within this book are for clarifying purposes only and are the owned by the owners themselves, not affiliated with this document.

Step 1: How to Understand the Suffering

To get **over** a broken heart, you need to first completely understand exactly what you're dealing with. After all, wouldn't you do the same if you somehow contracted a disease that you knew nothing about? Or if you were buying a house in a neighborhood that you weren't intimately familiar with?

We tend to spend our time and resources understanding things that are so external to our fundamental nature, yet spend the same amount of time ignoring what makes us who we are. This may sound cheesy and mushy, but we *are* dealing with emotions here.

In a series of groundbreaking experiments in 2006 involving MRI scans of brains of people in love, a leading anthropological expert on the subject of the biology of love and attraction, Dr. Helen Fisher, conclusively proved what country music and emo songs had been claiming for a long time: love is a drug.

Now, what that essentially means is that trying to act like a stoic, and strong-arming your way to healing cold turkey would work about as effectively for you as it would for a severe junkie going through withdrawal. If you feel like you have a built-in aversion to dealing with your emotions, well, tough! You have to do it nonetheless, especially if you don't want to mentally and emotionally scar yourself for life over someone who's no longer even a part of it. Whether that was your choice or your ex's is completely and entirely immaterial.

When we suffer from a broken heart, simply "bucking up" and "acting tough" aren't enough, because the pain we feel isn't just in our heads. It's actually partly physical and physiological as well. We undergo much of the same symptoms as drug withdrawal: fatigue, loss of appetite, and cravings. So, stop telling yourself that it's all in your head, and that toughing it out alone is going to work, because when that dam of stoicism breaks, it might end up doing a lot more harm than the original source of the pain.

Step 2: How to Break Away, and Why You Must

If a relationship truly mattered, then it's completely immaterial if you were the one breaking up or being broken up with. The first response from the brain after a small amount of time is pretty much the same in either case: denial. You've invested so much time, effort, affection, into this relationship and the other person, so your brain tries to tempt you into going back for more. But, just like someone trying to quit drugs or smoking, you need to break away.

Stop trying to stay friends. While I have nothing against people who may (pretend to) make this work, I can truthfully say I've never seen it happen in real life, especially if both people had a strong bond or intense feelings while in the relationship. Most people who successfully manage to do so after breaking up are usually in one of two scenarios — they realize they had overhyped what they felt all along during the relationship, or one of the two of them is lying their butts off about being okay with it being over. Sooner or later, one of the two trying to be friends will want more, and the whole messy cycle will start all over again. It's not healthy. It's the equivalent of turning your dead pet goldfish into a pendant and wearing it around your neck, while telling everyone you know that you don't even miss it.

Cut off contact completely. Remove them from your social networks and other related digital arenas. Don't go to parties of their best friends just to show up your ex or to play a game of chicken to see who backs off and admits first that they can't live without the other. Take your ego and pride out of it altogether, and concentrate on doing what's most healthy for you: letting go.

In addition to cutting them from your social networking sites, don't post or discuss details of your breakup. Don't post sad breakup poetry or selections of breakup songs. I can assure you, there will come a day when you'll look back and face-palm yourself for it. Even in the short term, it's pointless airing out your dirty laundry in public forums. The ones who care about you would get to know of it from you anyway, so why post your miseries for the twisted viewing pleasures of random people who would then laugh at the same?

But, the bigger goal of cutting your ex from every avenue of your life is to cut off that hope inside you that things will go back to how they were before the breakup. Trying to repair a relationship that's broken down to this extent is like trying to superglue a broken glass pitcher—no matter how pretty the end result may be after the repairs, it'll never be as whole or strong as it used to be. If love is truly like a drug, then any reason your brain may be seductively whispering to you which may bring you in contact with your ex, whether in the context of love or hate, is just another attempt at getting a high from that drug.

If you're one of the people who think that sticking around in the daily lives of their exes, regardless of the pain you feel, is **noble** of you in some way (???), then you must be into some weird venues of sadistic self-abuse. I strongly urge that you re-examine your motives and stop lying to yourself.

Also, if you keep thinking of ways to contact your ex in order to get closure, you need to know right now that not a single answer they can give you will be good enough. Nothing that they say will ease the pain or clear your confusion. Only you can give yourself closure, not the other person. The sooner you understand and accept this, the happier your life will become, and the quicker too.

Step 3: How to Let Yourself Feel

Give yourself a break. Most people act like going through a breakup and moving on is like going to the store and getting themselves a different brand of soap. There's no shame in feeling hurt after a breakup regardless of how good or bad the partner or the relationship may have been.

If you're reading this book then, as I mentioned before, you're already looking for a way to move on. Somewhere, you've already realized that this relationship was not the best thing for you, whether you consciously accept it or not. The pain that you're still feeling may be less about the ex and more about what they or the relationship *symbolized*: stability, normality, affection, and camaraderie. These feels are an enormous investment of your life, identity, and love. The co-routines that relationships invariably build are ones that form your life. So, if you agree with me, and accept that it's the ideals of a relationship you miss, rather than that relationship itself, with that specific person, then the best thing for you is to sort through these post-breakup issues quickly so that you can move on to a healthy and happy bond with a deserving partner.

After a breakup, we tend to overly romanticize the good parts and gloss over the bad. It's not something we do intentionally; it's something that our brain does to let us justify going back for another hit from that drug.

So, good or bad, whatever your experience in the relationship and with your ex may have been, stop trying to be a Hollywood hero who has been shot ten times and stoically walks a thousand and one miles to die in the arms of his lover.

You're hurting, and that's *okay*. Whether you're a guy or a girl, let yourself feel it all. Scream into a pillow, cry if you feel like it, and I promise you it will pass. Besides, it's already scientifically proven that a good scream works as excellent pain relief and helps lighten your mental load as well. So, get a good scream going now, and let that pain you're feeling out, because tiny frustrations can push the buttons until it can't be bottled up anymore.

What you *don't* want to do is close yourself off to the love and affection of other people in your life who care about you.

Step 4: How to Stop Blaming Yourself

It's become a sad habit among most people going through a breakup to blame themselves alone for the entire destruction of the relationship, and it may surprise you to learn that this isn't exclusively in people who were broken up with. Both people tend to do this. As the old adage goes, you can't clap with one hand.

No matter how bad things may have been, both people *are* responsible to some degree. But, there's absolutely no scenario in which it was your fault alone to bear. We tend to over-analyze issues after going through a breakup, believing that if we'd done a little more or a little less, things may have ended up differently.

I'm not going to lie to you about this: if the two of you had worked on the relevant issues, it *may* have ended up differently, but also, *it may have not*. You'll never know for sure. What doesn't change though, is that if the breakup has come to pass, one of the two cares less about sticking around and solving the problem than the other. So, stop blaming yourself for everything, stop glossing over your ex's faults and flaws, and stop clinging on to an idea and bond that is now dead.

In fact, what I would have you do **right now**, at this very moment in time, is take a piece of paper and write three things about your ex that were absolutely awful. Stop trying to be polite, and making light of their flaws. You aren't in the relationship anymore.

Now, on a separate piece of paper, write down three of the best qualities about yourself that you bring to the table in any relationship.

If you can't seem to think of them all, I'll give you some time and you and revisit this after the next tip.

Step 5: How to Let Out Aggression, then Calm Down

When people face troubles getting over a breakup, they get advice like "do yoga to calm down." But, really, in the first few stages after a breakup, that rarely ever works. In fact, the quietness of yoga just ends up with us running the reels of the relationship through our mind the whole time, and you end up feeling even more aggravated than before you started.

So, this is what I want you to do. If you go to a gym that may have a punching bag, go use it. Even if you never have before. And again, this applies to both guys and girls. Go punch the living daylights out of it. If you don't, then fashion a homemade punching bag out of pillows and use it. Hop on the treadmill and run as hard as you can. Or go for a short, yet vigorous run outside. But whatever physical exercise you do, perform it aggressively, as if you're Rocky prepping for the next title match and each second of training matters. Get that anger out because no matter what you tell yourself, there's a lot of it in there, and you'd be surprised by how much of it there is once you give it a healthy outlet.

Tackle things like meditation only **after** you've expended that aggression and pent up frustration inside you. Otherwise it will just keep playing that same old broken record in your mind that turns everything into a pity party.

If you believe that you've sufficiently vented enough of your anger today to let you calm down, even if just for the moment, go for it. Here's what I want you to do. Pick a place that's comfortable. It doesn't have to be the floor, and you don't have to sit cross-legged. Meditation is a state of mind that's best achieved when you're comfortable. Sit in whatever pose is most comfortable for you, and then close your eyes and start breathing deeply in and out.

Count each breath and only after your breathing has stabilized enough, think about your relationship. But this time, I don't want you to play some skewed tribute reel in your head. I want you to picture the moments that cause the most pain and pleasure out of it all, and with each scene or moment, tell yourself that *it's over* and that *you accept that, and your life will get better with each day from here on out* while you're breathing out. Even if your mind may struggle against the concept, push yourself through it, but not for longer than fifteen minutes or so. If you feel like you're getting aggravated again, get up and pursue something else that will let you expend that rage.

But, once you successfully get through it and get up, after having told yourself a number of times that you accept that it's over, you'll feel like a heavy burden has been lifted off your shoulders.

This is not necessarily a one-time thing though. Depending on how intense your emotions may have been and the hurt that you feel, you may have to make a cycle of releasing your aggression and then meditating to accept the current point in life you're at.

Now that you've gone through the aggression and meditation exercises for today, I want you to take out that paper again and list three more things about yourself that you love or that are purely awesome and that you bring to each relationship. Every time you get up from a bout of meditation, whether successful or not, I want you to pull this list back out and add three more things about yourself that a relationship partner would be lucky to have

While every "relationship guru" harps on and on about **loving yourself**, this is the best way to go about it. While loving yourself is important advice, giving it to someone who's hurting is about as useful as telling a person with weight issues that they need to eat less and exercise more. Generic and sound, but rarely helpful without specific direction. Every time you feel low about yourself, bring this list back out and read through it. And add to it whenever you think of something new. Also add to it any skill sets that you excel at, or cool hobbies that you indulge in. Once this list starts to grow, title it at the top *"My Inventory of Awesomeness."*

Step 6: How to Fill the Void

In the meantime, you also have to contend with another thing. While in a relationship, your activities and daily schedule were likely planned according to the needs of two people. Now, after the breakup, you may find vacuums or voids in your life that you may feel drag you down. *This* is where keeping busy becomes useful — not as a way to avoid what you're feeling, but as a way to move on since you're facing your emotional needs every day and dealing with them in a healthy fashion.

The best advice I can give you here is as you're out of the relationship, do all the things that you loved to do but didn't because of your ex. Beyond that, go through all the movies, shows, books, etc. that you'd always wanted to watch or read, but never found the time for, or that you didn't do because your ex didn't want to. Treat this as a time of "I can finally do exactly what I want to, because he's not around anymore."

If you're doing this after the aggression exercises and meditation, you're no longer avoiding your mental health issues, but starting to celebrate your own *"Me Time"* again after having been in the confines of a relationship. Staying busy now becomes a simple matter of filling an arithmetic need of the time left over that you would otherwise have devoted to your ex's needs or wishes. Pick up new hobbies, learn new languages — use this newfound time to expand your **Inventory of Awesomeness**.

Step 7: How to Address Your Flaws

Once your inventory is starting to build up, and you feel more confident about your own personality, there's nothing wrong with thinking about over what went wrong from your end in the last relationship. Don't use it as an excuse to indulge in self-pity or deny your own involvement in any wrongdoing. Use this exercise objectively to gain a deeper understanding of your approach toward different situations in a relationship, and understand how you could improve your outlook to make yourself a better partner for your next relationship.

Under no circumstances should you turn to drugs or alcohol to avoid dealing with any negative feelings. They only suppress the symptoms in the short term and do nothing to solve the problem itself.

Also, the habit of turning to chemicals to solve your problems isn't just a bad one because of the dangers of addiction, it pretty much renders you incapable of being able to face troubles in the future, regardless of your age or phase in life. Face your troubles head-on and get through them once and for all rather than suppressing them and carrying that baggage for the rest of time.

Think of this time as an opportunity to identify your own flaws, and then work on them to ensure you don't drag them into your next relationship, so that it has a greater chance of success. Use this time wisely, and you'll be glad you did later on.

Step 8: How to Get Your Social Life Back on Track

Normally, when we get into a relationship, we tend to lose track of our own individual social life and outlying friends and acquaintances. We spend less and less time away from our partner.

Once your relationship is over, it's perfectly normal to want to lay low and avoid contact with the world. It's quite understandable, and in small bursts, it isn't wrong to indulge this wish. But, by small bursts I mean three to four days at most.

But once that period is over, force your butt out of bed, go take a shower, and get dressed up and looking good! Call up your close friends and go out with them. There's nothing wrong with having a few drinks, but make sure of a few things:

First, remind yourself of all the good you've done while following this guide in the past few days, and that you don't want to undo all that work. This outing is a rest and unwinding period that you've earned, because you've followed the advice so well. Limit yourself to a few drinks and nurse and enjoy them while you catch up with your friends. After all, it's the company that provides the balm and that you're here to enjoy, not the booze.

Second, give your phone over to a trusted friend or ask someone to keep an eye out and make sure that—under no circumstances—should you drunk-text or drunk-dial your ex. That's a situation that lands you in a mess that's worse than being back at square one.

If you don't feel like going out to a bar, then think of some other activity that you would enjoy doing with your friends instead. Get the gang together and go out dancing instead, or take a snow-skiing trip, or whatever else strikes your fancy. You can also take up new hobbies together with friends, and expand your ***Inventory of Awesomeness*** with good company.

In case most of your friends were common company with your ex, the best advice I have is to search and join hobby classes, which are offered everywhere, regardless of country and continent. Not only will you have fun learning cool, new things, but you're sure to expand your social circles while doing so.

This will give you access to people and experiences that weren't shared with your ex or who wouldn't remind you of your emotional history in every meeting. It's the cleanest way for you to get a fresh start in your life and gives you a healthy outlet to turn to when you feel like everyone who shared your emotional past is dragging you down.

Meeting other new people and gaining new perspectives from them while learning new skills or acquiring new hobbies will also let you grow as a person and keep you from stagnating or wallowing in self-pity. It should effectively remind you of how awesome you are as your own person even without the added attachment of another being on you at all times.

If, at this point, you feel like you're ready for some intimate companionship or going out on a date, give yourself some room and indulge yourself within reason. Certainly never do it in a state of intoxication, or in a state of emotional distress. And if a casual acquaintance were to develop into something more, then consider whether you're in a healthy state of mind and ready to accept it.

Also, if you've reached this point, congrats! The worst of the phases have passed, and you're well on your way to having successfully healed your broken heart!

Conclusion

While there may be plenty of other tips that work for individuals, the points that I've listed above can help everyone, without exception, to get over the pain of a breakup sooner and faster than you may believe, and with a better approach to future relationships. If you breezed through the book without following the tips, then I suggest you go back through it again and follow it like an instruction manual, not skipping a single step.

Here's a recap on the most important things to remember:

- A breakup is, in no way, a commentary on your self-worth.

- It can never be entirely your fault that the breakup came to pass. But, the best thing to do is to stop caring about assigning blame, cut off unhealthy hope, and concentrate on moving in one direction only: forward.

- Stay away from your ex until you feel there are no longer any lingering feelings from your end or anything other than an entirely platonic approach to the interaction. Be honest with yourself about this.

- Don't stop yourself from feeling, now or in the future. Great rewards come with great risks, and there's no reward greater than a fulfilling and happy lifelong relationship with a deserving partner.

- Don't bottle your anger or sorrow. The punching bag and a pillow to scream in are fast solutions for stuff you keep bottled up inside unnecessarily.

- Don't turn to drugs or alcohol or other such venues to mask your pain.

- Don't push away people who are concerned about you, but don't talk about your breakup every chance you get either. When you come out of it all, you'll find that the latter results in awkward relations with the people whose ears you talked off on the matter, unless they're your very closest friends.

- Keep working on your *Inventory of Awesomeness*. It will help you evolve socially, professionally, and personally. Look at this as a time for personal growth and development.

- Don't hook up while drunk or otherwise intoxicated. If you're genuinely attracted to someone, the attraction won't disappear when you're sober, and the experience might be even more fulfilling.

Finally, I'd like to thank you for purchasing this book! If you found it helpful, I'd greatly appreciate it if you'd take a moment to leave a review on Amazon. Thank you, and best wishes for a future full of love and happiness.

Made in the USA
Middletown, DE
31 August 2021